A HILARIOUS GUIDE
FOR TRAVELING KIDS

BY
CHRISTINE POWELL AND MICAH TANNENBAUM

To Quinn,
I hope you have fun with my
travel book. I have a feeling you
will come up with lots of ideas
of your own! With love,
Christine Powell
11/2022

A HILARIOUS GUIDE FOR TRAVELING KIDS

TABLE OF CONTENTS

INTRODUCTION

As many parents and grandparents know, a very bright, energetic 9-year-old can be a handful when traveling.

It was Christmas time when Micah (9 years old), his mom, and I, his grandmother (Grammie), had traveled to New York City to have High Tea at the Plaza Hotel. We were seated at the beautiful table when Micah decided to lie across the seating area and play under the table. This is not acceptable behavior in a restaurant, so we talked about how he should behave. At that moment our book was inspired and created.

I came up with the proper behavior responses (A) and Micah.... well, he had fun coming up with the remaining responses. (B, C, and D).

Oh, and E, I left blank because maybe you have your own suggestion for proper behavior.

HAVE FUN DECIDING WHICH ANSWER IS THE BEST ANSWER!

BEHAVIOR KEY

A = PROPER BEHAVIOR AT ALL TIMES

B = BORDERLINE BAD BEHAVIOR

C = NEVER DO THIS

D = BAD/HORRIBLE BEHAVIOR

E = YOUR OWN SUGGESTIONS

CHAPTER 1: RESTAURANT BEHAVIOR

1. How do you behave in a fancy restaurant?

A. Sit in your chair in an upright position at all times, use your inside voice and talk nicely with the people around you, and look them in the eye when talking.

B. Lay on couch and ignore the people you're sitting with.

C. Lay on the couch, yell for food, and stick out your tongue at the waiter.

D. Throw your utensils at the closest people.

E.

2. If the lady at the next table stands up on her high heels and falls on you, what do you do or say?

A. "Oh, miss, how can I help you?" And then help her up.

B. Push her off and say, "EXCUSE YOU"!

C. Poke her with your fork and say, "WELL DONE!"

D. Just yell, "Get off of me"!

E.

3. **If someone at the table farts loudly what should you do or say?**

   A. Nothing, and just pretend you didn't hear it, and move on.

   B. Wrinkle your nose and say really loud, "EW........"

   C. Loudly exclaim "What did you eat for breakfast? It smells like something died in your intestines."

   D. Run screaming and yelling from the restaurant saying, "That Guy Farted!"

   E.

4. **If there is an earthquake during your meal, what should you do?**

   A. Stay calm, check the situation, and see how you can help.

   B. Pick up things that have dropped on the floor and put them in your pocket.

   C. Scream and cry as loud as you can.

   D. If the earth has opened up, push people in.

   E.

5. If there is a power outage and all the lights go out, what should you do?

    A. Stay calm and think about where the closest exits are.

    B. Eat things off your neighbor's table.

    C. Scream at the top of your lungs, "I Can't See You Mommy."

    D. Hide as many purses and wallets as you can.

    E.

CHAPTER 2: BEHAVIOR WHEN GOING SIGHTSEEING

1. You are on your way to see a special site. How do you behave?

    A. Walk or ride quietly, so the adults can concentrate on getting there.

    B. If walking, hang on to your mother's arm and whine.

    C. Dart out in front of traffic as a distraction when you are bored.

    D. Let go of your mother's hand and run in the opposite direction.

    E.

2. What to do when you are at the site?

    A. Always listen to your parent, hold their hand if they tell you to, and listen to what they want to teach you.

    B. Let go of their hand and run.

    C. Close your eyes and try to walk without running into a wall.

    D. Let go of their hand and choose another mother.

    E.

3. What do you do when you meet someone new?

A. Stop, look them in the eye, shake their hand, and say, "How do you do? Nice to meet you!"

B. Don't look at them, roll your eyes, and walk past them.

C. Run, because you really don't want to meet them.

D. Handshake with your right hand and kick them with your left foot.

E.

4. How should you behave in a taxicab or Uber?

A. Sit quietly, look out the window at the new sights.

B. Pull your beanie over your eyes and moan, "I have to pee."

C. Continue kicking the back of the driver's seat.

D. Cover the driver's eyes and see where he goes.

E.

CHAPTER 3: HOTEL BEHAVIOR

1. What do you do when you first arrive at your hotel?

   A. Follow the grown-ups and walk behind them to your hotel room.

   B. Swing through the revolving doors and don't stop.

   C. Immediately jump on the nicely made beds and try to touch the ceiling.

   D. Call room service and tell them it's for the room next door.

   E.

2. You are in your hotel room, and you are very bored, what could you do?

   A. Do your homework if you brought it, read your book, play a game on an iPad, or ask a grown-up to play a game with you.

   B. Run around the room speaking loudly, annoying the grown-ups.

   C. Bang on the neighbor's wall to borrow some toothpaste.

   D. Turn on all the water faucets full blast, so the water overflows on to the floor.

   E.

3. What should you do if you get stuck in the elevator?

A. Try to remain calm and push the call button on the control panel for help.

B. Start to scream loudly until someone slaps you.

C. Lay down in the elevator and pound on the floor.

D. Pick up the closest person and bang their head against the roof until you can get out.

E.

4. What should you do if you get lost in the hotel?

A. Go to the front desk, tell them you lost your parents, and tell them your name.

B. Stand in one place and cry your eyes out.

C. Walk out the front door and get on a double-decker bus.

D. Go to the front desk, find the deskman, pull his tie until his chin hits the counter, and tell him your problem.

E.

5. What should you do when you can't fall asleep in your hotel room?

A. Put your head on the pillow, ask mom for some earplugs, and close your eyes.

B. Throw all covers off, put your head under your pillow, and sing "Baby Shark" as loud as you can.

C. Wet a washcloth and wring it out over your mother's face.

D. Sneak out the door, knock loudly, and when your parent answers, say "Trick or Treat, smell my feet, give me something good to eat."

E.

CHAPTER 4: BEHAVIOR IN SNOW CONDITIONS

1. How do you dress when going to play in the snow.

    A. Wear a warm jacket, warm pants, a hat, snow boots, and, of course, mittens.

    B. Wear a tank top, shorts, and a warm Warriors hat.

    C. Wear a hula skirt, puka shells, flip flops, and a beanie.

    D. Wear your mom's underwear and put on suntan lotion.

    (E.) Wear a beanie, earmuffs, scarf, a warm jacket, warm pants, snow boots

2. How do you behave now that you are at the ski resort?

    A. Follow your mom and dad and listen to instructions.

    B. Put on your skis quickly and leave your family in the dust.

    C. Jump on the chair lift without skis and then run down the hill.

    D. Take off one ski, when your mom bends over push her down the hill with your ski.

    E.

3. How to behave on a ski lift?

A. Sit still look at the beautiful view and position your poles away from the person sitting next to you.

B. Burp twice and sing God Bless America as loud as you can.

C. Stand up while on the ski lift with your skis on and swing the chair back and forth

D. Take your skis off and push them down the hill aiming for the people below.

E.

4. Lunchtime behavior at the ski lodge.

A. Take off your skis and place your poles neatly outside of lodge.

B. Ski into lodge and yell cheeseburger and fries.

C. Finish your soda and cut in line in front of everyone for a refill.

D. Take as many bags of chips as you can, stomp on them and throw them at your friends.

E.

CHAPTER 5: BEHAVIOR WHEN AT THE BEACH

1. What do you wear to the beach?

    A. Bathing suit, flip-flops, and a baseball cap, and bring sunscreen, a beach towel, and a tasty lunch.

    B. Cowboy boots, a funny hat, a wool sweater, and a gorilla mask.

    C. Thermal underwear

    D. Your mother's fancy dress and her high heels.

    E.  Bathing suit, a light jacket, flipflops, sunglasses

2. Where do you put your beach towel?

    A. Next to your parents or the people you are with.

    B. Next to the ocean, so it will get taken away.

    C. Lay your towel on any stranger closest to you and run away.

    D. Run around the beach and whip people with your towel.

    E.  lie it down in a cozy spot

3. When your parents fall asleep sunbathing what should you do?

    A. Play quietly near them.

    B. Eat everything in the picnic basket.

    C. Kick sand in their faces, then run.

    D. Find a boat and sail away.

    E.

4. What do you do when swimming in the ocean?

    A. Never turn your back to the ocean or go in any further than your parents tell you.

    B. Close your eyes and run as fast as you can into the ocean.

    C. Push your mother in and then hang onto her neck while swimming.

    D. Swim way out there, scream "Shark!," and pretend you are drowning.

    E.  splash around

CHAPTER 6: BEHAVIOR WHEN AT THE MOVIES

1. What do you do when you first arrive at the movies?

    A. Go get snacks at the counter with your mom or dad.

    B. Run behind the snack counter and help yourself to candy and popcorn.

    C. Cut in front of everybody in line, so you can be first.

    D. Go take money out of the cash register and stash it in your pocket for later.

    E.

2. What do you do now that you have your snacks?

    A. Walk alongside your parent and find the right movie theater.

    B. Run up and down the aisles looking for the perfect seat.

    C. Throw popcorn in the seat you want to sit in.

    D. Find the perfect seat and pull the person out, so you can be very comfortable.

    E.

3. The movie has started how shall we behave?

A. Sit quietly and watch the show.

B. After your soda, burp loudly least ten times in a row.

C. Take your guinea pig out of your backpack and let him roam free, while you are enjoying the show.

D. Pull the persons hair that is sitting in front of you as hard as you can, because they will never know it's you.

E.

4. What to do when leaving the theater now that the movie is over?

A. Walk alongside your parents commenting on the movie.

B. Dart in and out of the crowds and avoid your parents.

C. Tell the people waiting in line that the movie stinks.

D. Run as fast as you can into the street into oncoming traffic.

E.

CHAPTER 7: BEHAVIOR AT YOUR GRANDMOTHER'S HOUSE

1. **What to do when you first arrive at Grammie's house?**

   A. Run into house, give Grammie a huge hug and kiss, and tell her how much you missed her.

   B. Run into house, climb onto the sofa, and continue jumping until it's dinner time.

   C. Continue bouncing the beach ball and throwing it against the wall until the pictures fall off the wall.

   D. Drop all your luggage and belongings in the front entranceway, so everyone coming in after you will trip.

   E.

2. **How to behave at Grammie's dinner table?**

   A. Fold your freshly washed hands and bow your head to participate in a prayer of thanks.

   B. Wipe your nose on your sleeve and ask for the mashed potatoes.

   C. Chew with your mouth wide open, while eating your asparagus and drool.

   D. Turn to your cousin sitting next to you and smash that pie in her face.

   E.

3. How do we behave at bedtime at Grammie's house?

A. Brush your teeth, get ready for bed, and get your favorite book.

B. Put toothpaste on the wall, smear it around, and see if she notices.

C. Tell Grammie you are going to sleep now, then sneak into the kitchen and eat all the cookies in the cookie jar.

D. Unplug all electrical outlets in the house and see Grammie go crazy.

E.

4. How should you behave when you are spending a day with your Grammie?

A. Plan and enjoy the day together.

B. Hide your only pair of shoes, so you don't have to go shopping at Nordstroms.

C. Continue playing on your iPad, and do not listen to a word Grammie is saying.

D. Destroy Grammie's plans for you and make her cry.

E.

5. How to behave when meeting Grammie's friends.

    A. Shake their hands and say, "Nice to meet you."

    B. Hide in the corner and shout, "Howdy!"

    C. Turn the music up to full blast and pretend you are a rock star!

    D. Climb in the tree and dump a pitcher of lemonade on everyone, then run from Grammie.

    E.

CHAPTER 8: HOW TO BEHAVE AT THE AIRPORT

1. What should you do when you first get to the airport?

A. Stay close to your parents and follow them with your suitcase.

B. Run around while your mom is trying to check you in and see if she can catch you.

C. Stand on the suitcase scale and see how much you weigh.

D. Ride around on the baggage carousel, sit on a suitcase and pretend you're the president of the airlines.

E. fart in public and then blame the flight attendent

2. What do you do while waiting in the security check line with your parents?

A. Stand quietly paying attention to your parents and moving through the line with all the other people.

B. Stand still and do not move as the line moves ahead and block all the people behind you.

C. Run through security check and say, "I have no jellybeans," and keep running.

D. When they ask you to take your shoes off, take off your pants.

E.

3. You have 2 hours before the plane leaves and now you're hungry. What should you do?

A. Tell your parents you're really hungry and would like a plain bagel with strawberry cream cheese.

B. Moan and whine and see if they can guess what's wrong with you.

C. Leave the family in search of that bagel.

D. Use mom's cell phone to order a quick bagel delivery to Gate 24.

(E.) go get Food

4. You have boarded the plane and you are ready for take off, how should you behave?

(A.) Fasten your seatbelt and make sure you have your books and games where you can reach them.

B. Keep kicking the back of the chair in front of you.

C. Throw all of your M&M's into the aisle so everyone can have one.

D. Stick your legs out into the aisle and see what happens.

E.

CHAPTER 9: HOW TO BEHAVE AT THE LIBRARY

1. **What do you do when you first walk into the library?**

   A. As you walk in, say hello and smile at the friendly librarian.

   B. Ignore the librarian completely, especially when she says hello.

   C. Walk into the library with your bathing suit on and your beach umbrella open.

   D. Jump over the librarian's desk and tell her you are replacing her.

   E.

2. **What kind of voice do you use while in the library?**

   A. It's best if there is no talking at all while in the library, or use a very soft voice.

   B. Talk normal so all the people around you can hear you.

   C. Find a seat and belt out "Jingle Bells", so people know you are there.

   D. Burp ten times in a row while you sit down comfortably to read your book.

   E.

3. What do you do after you have found your book?

A. Give the librarian your library card, so she can check it out for you.

B. Give the librarian your empty potato chip bag from lunch.

C. Once you have found your book, throw it across the room, so the librarian can check your book out.

D. Push one of the standing bookcases to see if they fall like dominoes.

E.

4. How do you take care of your library book?

A. Take good care of this book because you are just borrowing it.

B. Sit on it on the way home in the car.

C. Leave the book at your neighbor's house, so the family can read it.

D. Use the book as a baseball bat in the house and hit everything with it.

E.

CHAPTER 10: HOW TO GET READY FOR YOUR TRIP

1. **How do you pack your suitcase?**

    A. Pull your suitcase out of closet and put your pants, tee shirts, toothbrush, comb, shoes, and socks in it.

    B. Pull your suitcase out of the closet, sit on it, and dream about tomorrow.

    C. Throw in your basketball and pictures of your 3 dogs.

    D. Take all your clothes and sneak them in with other family members.

    E. put your clothes in the suitcase and then roll it to your front door

2. **How can you help your mom and dad get ready for your trip?**

    A. Do what they ask because they need your help right now.

    B. Hide all day so they can't find you.

    C. Invite lots of your friends over to bake a chocolate cake.

    D. Put the cat in mom's suitcase.

    E.

3. Time to get in the car, what do you do?

    A. Grab your suitcase and put it in the trunk.

    B. Run into the house for one more thing, then hide again.

    C. Chase the car because they left without you.

    D. Climb on the car roof when no one is looking and sit on the roof on the way to the airport.

    E.

TRAVELER

Place for your photo here

Your name here

Quinn

CHAPTER 11: WRITE YOUR OWN TRAVEL QUESTIONS AND ANSWERS

QUESTION

#1...

    A.

    B.

    C.

    D.

    E.

QUESTION

#2...

    A.

    B.

    C.

    D.

    E.

CONCLUSION

If you have decided that (A) is the right answer for all the questions, then you are ready to travel!

Have a great trip and always remember to use good manners and be kind and considerate wherever you go!!!

HAPPY TRAVELS......

ABOUT THE AUTHORS

CHRISTINE POWELL

Christine Powell has had many roles throughout her life, a sister, daughter, wife, mother, grandmother, and a beloved friend to many. Professionally, she worked in the health care industry as a Radiological Technologist, from which she recently retired.

But her most important role is that of a mother of three wonderful girls and five amazing grandchildren. Her love for all of them is boundless, and it was that love that inspired her to write this book, which she hopes will benefit not only her grandchildren, but your children and grandchildren, as well. Christine resides in Danville, CA.

MICAH TANNENBAUM

Micah Tannenbaum is now a teenager, and his robust love of life and endless energy at the age of nine were the inspiration for this book. All the content was a direct result of his amusing behaviors and his and Grammie's hilarious sense of humor. As he has matured, Micah is achieving academic excellence and is a talented basketball player with dreams of the NBA. Micah resides in Los Angeles, California.

CONTACT INFORMATION

Christine Powell
Danville, California
powellchristine007@gmail.com

Made in the USA
Las Vegas, NV
12 October 2022